Hurricane Matthew: Through the Storm

Sonya McGirt, MSW, MA

ISBN:1540661962
ISBN-13:9781540661968

DEDICATION

I dedicate this book to my hometown (Lumberton) and all the residents of Robeson County. We will look back ten years from now and we will be proud of how we handled this disaster. God was with us and will be with us as we move forward.

ACKNOWLEDGMENTS

I would like to acknowledge all the individuals who allowed me to use these photos. Jeanna Britt, Brianna Townsend, Trevor and Gabbie Chavis, Joanie Walters and Kris Warwick

BEFORE THE STORM

"PRAY CONTINUALLY" 1 THESSALONIANS 5:17

After the Storm

"Fear thou not; for I am with thee: be not dismayed; for I am thy God: I will strengthen thee; yea, I will help thee; yea, I will uphold thee with the right hand of my righteousness." Isaiah 41:10

ABOUT THE AUTHOR

Sonya McGirt was born and raised in North Carolina. She lives with her husband, Chris, and their three daughters: Ceirra, Madison, and Gracelyne. Sonya has a Master's degree in Social Work from USC Columbia and an undergraduate degree from UNCP. She recently obtained her second Master's degree in Organizational Management. She has over ten years of experience working within the Mental Health field, and runs a nonprofit agency, Crossroads Christian Counseling Center, which assists those in need. She is also the author of the Children's book, Sam the Duck.

www.ingramcontent.com/pod-product-compliance
Lightning Source LLC
Chambersburg PA
CBHW060805290526

45792CB00005BA/1533